JOURNEY THROUGH
EXPERIENCE

JOURNEY THROUGH
EXPERIENCE

Poems

JOSEPH M. CODDINGTON

JOURNEY THROUGH EXPERIENCE
POEMS

iUniverse books may be ordered through booksellers or by contacting:

iUniverse
1663 Liberty Drive
Bloomington, IN 47403
www.iuniverse.com
1-800-Authors (1-800-288-4677)

ISBN: 978-1-5320-8148-4 (sc)
ISBN: 978-1-5320-8149-1 (hc)
ISBN: 978-1-5320-8147-7 (e)

Library of Congress Control Number: 2019912768

Print information available on the last page.

iUniverse rev. date: 02/27/2020

To my Father (now deceased),
To my Mother,
And to Iqbal

Contents

Joseph M. Coddington Biography

May 10, 1943 - January 26, 2017

Joseph Mark Coddington was born in 1943 to a middle class family in Susquehanna, Pennsylvania, and was the youngest of six siblings. When he was nine, his family moved to Binghamton, New York where he received his high school education at a Catholic Academy. After his high school education in 1960, he attended SUNY Oneonta college in Central New York for a year and left the college to join the Navy, following the path of his older brothers. The two years of Navy service opened a window to the outside world for Joseph and he aspired to explore it. After the service, he took off to Indiana to work and start his undergraduate study in English at Butler University, a private university in Indianapolis. In 1967 and at the end of two years at Butler, he transferred his courses credits to Indiana University in Bloomington to experience life in a large scenic campus with a large student population. At Indiana University, Joseph received his BA in English and his Master's degree in creative writing with honors. He dabbled with short stories, but his real focus and passion was poetry.

In 1970, he married a fellow student working for her Ph.D. in anthropology; both continued their education while working on campus and enjoying the busy environment of the university. The seventies were an era of advancement in personal computer technology that dominated the market and stirred an intellectual challenge on campuses to invest in computer studies for a better future. Joseph embraced the trend. He bought a computer to train himself to become a computer specialist. After graduation, he worked for the Federal Aviation Administration (FAA) center in Indianapolis as a computer analyst and programmer. Within a few years, he was transferred to the FAA center in New Jersey and then in Oklahoma. While still working for the FAA, he was sent to Amman, Jordan to help clear the problem the Jordanian government had with its central computer system.

In 1978, Joseph joined the International Mensa Chapter of Oklahoma. He produced its monthly newsletter where he published some of his articles and poems. This was a time Joseph and his wife reminisced about its intellectual and social activities and they gained valuable friendships and experience.

In 1987, Joseph left the FAA for California, the hub of computer technology, creativity and social change which he enjoyed. In California, he worked for the National Geological Survey in Menlo Park as a computer specialist for several years. He participated in some of their scientific expeditions when his computer proficiency was needed in the field. In California, he joined the San Francisco Mensa Chapter but had to leave it to concentrate on his work and other responsibilities. Later, Joseph bid farewell to the world of technology and joined NOVA, which is a national organization that assists and trains people for new careers at various levels. He enjoyed the human aspect of the job and the pleasure of helping others. At NOVA, he was appreciated for his "exceptional ability and his effective counseling and leadership."

During this period, Joseph's marriage was facing more difficulties which eventually led to separation in 1987 and ended with a divorce in 1992. In 2002, he married an assistant researcher at Stanford University working on primate's brain. Joseph continued his work at NOVA until he retired for serious health problems and passed away in January 2017.

As an individual, Joseph Coddington was compassionate and an ardent truth seeker, blessed with keen intellect and a sharp sense of humor. He loved challenges and winning. Adventures for him were means of self-discovery, learning, and enjoyment. He joined the Public Speaking club, Poetry Reading club, and as part of his love for sport, he joined skiing clubs whenever he lived in or near cold snowy areas. Politically, he was an active member of the Democratic party.

Joseph Coddington's adherence to idealism was stressful to him in time of adversity and change. Reading, writing, and other interests he had were a necessary distraction from the austerity of the daily routine. In his book *Journey through Experience*, he describes the pain and pleasure of his journey through life using his gift of language, sharply perceived vision, and powerful imagery. His poetry is universal in terms of its portrayal of the interaction of the self with the facts of nature and the complexity of human life blurred by illusions and the clash of the opposites that he so well expressed in his poems; "Rooted Continuity" and in "One Final Religious Experience".

Joseph Coddington's death cut short his journey of experience and was a great loss to his family and friends. His ashes are in small urns in the homes of those who loved him and cherish his memory.

Foreword

by
Margaret J. Howell

My acquaintance with Joseph Coddington began in 1964. We were students at Butler University in Indianapolis and later at Indiana University in Bloomington.

Joseph had started his university education after serving for two years in the United States Navy. Most of his poetry was written when he was young and a student. It was a time of drastic cultural change and a change in public affairs in the U.S.A., a time for shrugging off some of the verities or acquiring new alternatives. The influence of that time on Joseph is apparent in his rejection of the rituals of the Catholic church in which he had been brought up, and it might account for his pessimism. This is glanced at in "One Final Religious Experience" (6) and "Shapes in Shade" (13), two of his poems that record his religious confusion. In the first of these "the cup with wafers tips and falls". "A Christian weeps", "apostles forget the words of prayer and sleep", "crucifix cracks", the future dissolves in "lack love". The speaker goes into the "cold" and the "night".

Joseph kept quiet about his writing but was content it should be published after his death. We do not know what he thought of the new theories of poetry, but he did declare himself a modern man in conversation.

Few poems printed here comment on the actual art of writing; when they do they are enigmatic. In "Nutty-Putty Poet" (5) the speaker is a "whirling dervish of the words / always pregnant", "A Tree like a poem, must not think but be" (14). "For those who never flew I / describe the scene" (24) and once again "I'll tell the story / that I flew". These quotes suggest a poet can provide an experience and that he feels the urge to tell his tale. This impetus moves every authentic writer and it is germane to the theme of these poems.

The verses move in a rough biological sequence: from childhood, to adolescence, young manhood, the queries and experience of maturity, the death of his father, which "leaves only questions"(19), through to the last, ironically subtitled "A new Beginning"(25), which ends with the word "stops". The poems are written in free verse which had become very popular by the middle of the twentieth century. It gave up the strict forms, including rhyme, rhythm, and meter, and encouraged free choice of the subject matter. To compensate for the total or partial loss of the strict form, the free verse poets use punctuation, imposed patterns, internal rhyme, word order, arrangements on the page, sentence structure, and repetition of opening lines. Coddington used all these techniques with great efficiency. In "Time"(1), he compensates for the loss of rhyme and rhythm with punctuation, spacing, and repetition: "A time / A time". The repetition and elegant variation (saying the same thing in a different way) alludes eight times to snow (white flakes / snow flakes / cold / blizzard / frozen / drifts / snow.

Compensation for rhyme known as "alliteration" (repetition of initial consonants and vowels), and onomatopoeia (words imitating sounds) recurs in "Forever Emptiness"(16): "curtains of comfort", "curve elusive curtain". It is again in "One Final Religious Experience"(6) "final as forever falling... past pews / not forgiving my footsteps... a crucifix cracks". In "Gift" (18) "buzz-saw sun" and in "Harmonic Convergence" "Force without form"(25) announce the formation of a nova. In "Nutty-Putty Poet" (5) the speaker is "watching winter people, pouched and TV prone". The careful reader will find instances throughout of alliteration pointing up a reference. The "Nutty-Putty Poet" emphasizes or unifies groups of lines or creates a musical effect, setting up a kind of percussion. The sibilance (producing hissing sounds) in "Soft sounds shiver, / heard only by the inner ear / alert of sadness / and silence, / and things lost" of "Abstraction" (10) unites the lines and echoes the sense. The <u>w</u> is repeated throughout "The Memory Wood" (12) beginning "From window wedded eyes", and in "Questions for an Avid Motorcyclist"(19) the repetition of <u>st</u> (stillness, blister, stand, glisten, piston, breast) binds the opening lines and mimics the stuttering of an engine.

The poems are terse, the lines compressed and short. There is little room for internal rhyme. A few examples crop up: in "Rooted Continuity"(14) "the tree conveys to me", in "A Time"(1), "night . . . and sight" in "Need Help" (23) "to kill the chill", and in "Monkey-Hunger"(8), "of light and night". End rhymes are also rare. A particularly evocative use of onomatopoeia, in "Shapes in Shades"(13), "the sweeper comes / with its hissing", hints at the snake-like, especially as it is followed by the sinister and alliterative "mechanical mind". This poet has a good command of such devices, which carry suggestive associations with them, and he is sensitive to sound.

The regular metrical pattern may be broken up or altered for the sake of stress or emphasis which is rhetorical variation. This happens rather often in free verse, lacking as it does a consistent form. The fundamental rhythm of English is iambic, an unstressed followed by a stressed syllable. Poets can play with meter and reverse this, putting the stressed first, which is trochaic. Traces of both rhythms may be found, for example, in "Looking Glass Love"(7), "What kind / of think / ing brought / us here", "These are / days that / weigh as / heavy". Many lines are spondaic, with single syllables. From the same poems comes "have lost their back, / till now we look through". This meter treads heavily in the final lines of "Another Incident" (11), "to speak / my mind / and die"; and in "Harmonic Convergence" (25), all this / we call life / stops"; and most emphatically in "My Father Died"(17), "like a / shut Faucet / shut all day / but now / would have its say". It tolls grimly in "Forever Emptiness"(16), "at my ear, / the last sound / the last sound / I came to hear". It uplifts in "Wings" (24), "For those who did not try, I / will fly". In "My Father the Puppy Chaser" (2) the text makes the shape of the concrete steps. Setting the text in a block to the right shifts the idea, too, as in this poem The scene is moved from the steps to puppy freedom to the family asleep, oblivious of the fun. The poetic techniques are appropriate to the sense, and the diction exact.

The images and the theme are the most revealing of the poet's mind, suggesting melancholy throughout. "Time" (1) moves in three sections, from the pink-faced boy, rolling in snow through night and winter, to the end of the dreams, when lifeless frozen branches "puzzle us all" and then "the boy's footprints / are stolen by the drifts". This extends the meaning into a little allegory of life. The flakes sting, even the night is blown out by winter winds, and the snow becomes a hiding place "a blizzard not to play in". The drifts steal the boy's footprints. So life's promises are erased. The author here has control of his subject and presents an arresting idea graphically and through personification. The footprints are stolen. The snowdrifts are thieves, our traces are soon rubbed out, we are forgotten. There is a threat here, a darkness.

Snow has often meant death. It reappears in "Another Incident" (11) as the "white web-wind" where the speaker drifts cold. In "Gift"(18) the cat is cold / chill / cold". Pessimism is expressed through metaphor in "Manhood" (3) as "cricket in your house". Man's secrets like seeds underground never reach the surface, in "Secret"(4). In "Body Alone"(21) in a startling picture, the charred body was burned, melted "between snow sheets". And in the impersonal room are desk, unused chair, phone, Bible, and directory — shelved, new from disuse.

Poems 1 - 23 were composed while Joseph was in college. The remainder (24, 25, and 26) he wrote later. Unfortunately 26 is almost illegible, about half of it indecipherable, and it has therefore been decided not to attempt a re-construction. The title of the poem is "Touched, Turned on, Till Worn out". It is a coda to his life pilgrimage.

MARGARET J. HOWELL is a writer and teacher, retired, who lives in British Columbia. She is the author of *Byron Tonight: A Poet's Plays on the Nineteenth Century Stage*; *The House of Byron: A History of the Family from the Norman Conquest, 1066 - 1988* (with Violet W. Walker); *The Spirit of Understanding: English Literature in an Age of Confusion*; *A Meditation on King Richard III*; two pamphlets of poems: *The Seasons*, and *The Silence that Sings*; and of various articles and reviews.

1

A Time

At every angle
    white flakes sting my face.
Behind my shadow
    snowflakes sting the pink-faced boy
    with stringed gloves and earflaps
    waving everywhere at once
    as he, careless, rolls in snow.

–A time
  when night was
  (cold and black) made white
  then blown out of sight
  by winter winds.
–A time
  when fears were blurred
  by mother's velvet words
  as tears swept the boy's young cheeks
  to gather in the creases of a reappearing smile.

Dreams now are long years done.
  Snow has become a hiding place,
  a blizzard not to play in.
  Lifeless branches frozen on winter's sky
  puzzle us all,

      and the boy's footprints
      are stolen by the drifts.

2

My Father, the Puppy Chaser

In the early mornings
when we were still
secure in sleep,
my father would
free our puppies
from the house
to do
what puppies do
after being cardboard-boxed all night.
And run they would
downhill
past the flower-boxes on the wall,
past the wheels
of early moving Church Street cars,
past all impediments
but one:

      concrete steps
      (above the creek)
      which led

level by level
to puppy freedom   (and we,
                       still so sure
                       in dreamy sleep
                       that all things
                       were tranquil fur).

But Pop,
our puppy chaser,
always caught them
at the top
and returned them
to their box,
then went to work
upon the rails
before we even woke.

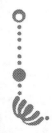

3

Manhood

When young,
   you seek it
   as you would
   a cricket in your house:
      in sensual ways–
         from side to side
         you swivel self to sound,
         to capture or to kill,
         but find
         this bug.
         elusive dark.

You're in! (you think)
when shipmates take you
to a bar
to drink beer or
whateverelse
will pass your lips.
So, you in dress whites,
spit-shined shoes, and
brand-new third-class crow
go to a bar,
throw "fucks" around

(like grapefruits at an orgy),
these into the smoke
which heavy, high and lazy, snakes,
muffles sounds of pool balls
as it loves the smell of beer.
She from out this swirling white
(like apparition) moves,
grabs your crotch,
bites your ear,
and takes you from the place.

And you
cannot speak
moving through that Lisbon street
nor upstairs in her room as
her folds receive
and vice-like hold,
her inside muscles craze
      (so this is, is...)
     and it comes
       as soft as sleep;

but then
in the dim bedroom afterlight
as you judge the ceiling lines,
look and wonder what
   the shape of manhood.

4

Secret

Man will have his secret bent:

seeds beneath the ground
that dormant
wait
the catalytic rain;

thoughts
that softly grow
below
the boundary line

behind
a placid face
(as lakes pretend
    while waiting wind).

5

Nutty-Putty Poet

I'm
   the nutty-putty poet
             on my block   silent
               watching winter people,
                   pouched and t.v. prone,
                spew out in sea-horse birth.
      From under winter cumber
                  (bumps and bulges)
          blossom shapes:
      spring tumbles out the best
                   in many things.

For
   I, the witty
             whirling dervish of the word,
      always pregnant,
           mother my balloons that
       spirit up on warm imagination
       and draw me up in sympathetic flight,
                   untouched,
                   untied.

And
    you in multi-colored spring clothes,
                              bright,
       yet ground-bound,
          must watch me float away.

6

One Final Religious Experience

Before the altar
bent
(on knees
   that bled
   from Mary's shrine
   to stark white cross
   to clot the dust of Portugal.

  I rise to go
  (the altar shifts,
  a cup with wafers
  tips and falls,
  hosts drop
  upon the cloth,
  a Christian weeps,
  apostles wake to pray,
  forget the words
  and sleep.

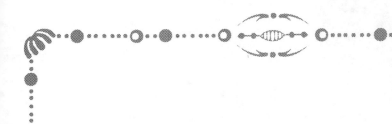

I turn
(final as forever falling
as continuous the aisle)
  and move past pews
  (not forgiving my footsteps
  as I pass,
  while candle-flames,
  all miniature hells of holiness
  catch and drag my face
  into many small departures;
  a crucifix cracks
  against the grain
  while somewhere mother,
  father cry my name
  into the image
  of my image;
  and at my back
  the future dissolves
  in the passive solution
  of lack-love).

    Before me,
    the Gothic doors (light)
    swing wide

(to winds
that blow always in,
now empty motion-mysteries),

and cold
I am
into night.

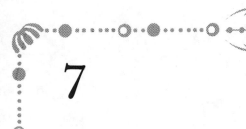

7

Looking-glass Love

These are days that weigh as heavy
    as graveyard ground;
and you stand straight
    though white and weathered,
and the season in your eyes
    will not change this year.
        The gathered clouds are anesthetized,
        their movement less
        than sounds of sand settling.
You breathe deep and utter broken sounds
    as if your tongue cannot reach your teeth.
Your words dribble
    water-over-rock-like,
while your smile lies
    above below trembling
like a prophecy
    near its time.

What kind of thinking brought us here–
    to this silent sickness?

Armed deeds flash unspoken fears
    as time breeds sad and sordid sights:
        we mirror ourselves
        (each the other's mirror)
        only to recoil
        reflected light refracted;
        with time the mirrors
        have lost their back,
        till now we look through
        looking-glass.

8

Monkey-Hunger

The mind touches no one
knowing no thing to touch.

Through window-square
past parallel bars
rides the day
on specks of dust
that catch and carry
bits of sun.
The absolute rite
of light and night
begins again;
through that square
past parallel bars:
three slash-like scars,
slender clock-work hands
which never meet the hour,
but travel down the door
along the floor
in separate motions merged.

And
     the man will not move
     against this movement,
     will not break this order
     of monotony,
     or speak
     to give the monkey
     at his back
     a chance
     to catch his words,
     crack their forms,
     and eat the contents
     (grinning).

So silent slides the day
till night shades the shadow
that (yet) defines this dark
where monkey-hunger hunches
expectantly.

9

Nothing To Say

I really have nothing
to say to you
except
perhaps
in a near vision
I saw
or thought I saw
from my stream bank
yours.

The young waters were clear
once
and swirled their skirts
before our eyes
and held their lines
with strong fluid sinews
before the rain
broke surface tension
upping the silt
to mar our gift–
I dared not cross.

I conjured a bridge
which sagged in the moving
relentless air;
the mortar faltered
and fell
and the stream swept it away.

Your bank went also
(or was it mine)
with its natural face
of green and brown
and you,
as love winds
caressed my mind
with anesthetic lips.

The rushing sounds
are mine alone
to hear,
unmistakably mine
as there are no others
to interfere:
    I go to them in their sweetness.

10

Abstraction: Mind on a Wave

Soft sounds shiver,
    heard only by the inner ear
       alert to sadness,
       and silence,
         and things lost.

It hears the breathing
    of patchwork skies,
      and dusk
        falling on a face
            upturned
              waiting.

At twilight,
    with gulls' wings pasted
      flat against the evening sky,
  lights
        (infinity bound)
      dart across darkening water
       to find their answer
         long after they pass me.

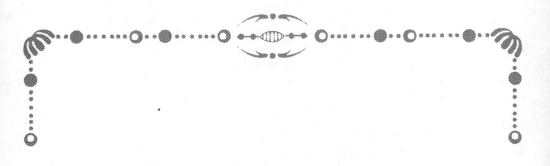

And then,
    when the clouds surround
      and capture a moon,
        playing with it,
          tossing it this way
             and that,

      at least
        I know
          that this
            has happened.

11

Another Incident

Caught
in the white web-wind
of winter's night,

I drift cold:
cold among the drifts
where I am sought.
When found
I am summoned
by his voice
fairy-light
(though sickness-sweet).

I am the victim
of his calling.
Its passion beats
on heavy heat
so
when he speaks,
words tremble
on my skin

and questions
stigmatize the air
as vermin leap
across my thoughts,
then grovel
at his cheek

to speak
my mind
and die.

12

The Memory-wood

From window-wedded eyes
   she watches simpli-
         city flow and go
           in moving-metal streets
               below,
  strands of hair, heat-wet
         limp at the temple
         to parody her wax-weariness
            with life
       that runs, then dries,
      then crumbles
      where it lies.

And she wonders at this now-world

not oak,
    that once grew tree-limb-close
  to stroke
      the hour
        and the glass
      of her day.

To close
those days
(of many trees)
she turned
her eyes
from lands of mist
and memories.

Now
the forest,
green
gone brown
to white,
walks
this woman's
day-time mind
to coax her
nearest
to its softer,
more brown
memory-wood
only
in the compromise
of the night.

13

Shapes in Shades

Winds blow
   and elastic trees
      move in slow sympathy.

A bell rings
   and the hour
      is that sound
         growing,
     a wafer which
            dissipates
              disintegrates
                and falls with dusk
                   to quiet streets.

The sweeper comes
   with its hissing
         mechanical mind
     and spins the streets
         from dust,

as the streetlights
   come off fog
      like small
         and separate dawns.

When rains fall,
   treaded-tires pass
                  to make miniature streams:
                              spreading,
                     then once again
                              one.

Before I came
   shape-like dogs
      crossed my way,
         then stood
            where I had gone.

And in translucent windows,
   dark eyes
      are darker eyes
         reflected.

14

Rooted Continuity

Before me here
   a tree that's always been a tree
in memory.
   But if I sit slow
         contemplative,
     I see
       a sketch
        arcing:
Black sap explodes
  along random unseen grooves,
    each drop streaking
     from the common source
      to seek some end of growing;
    each limb (dried)
     eddies the winds
      that send leaves
       crashing (loosed at once,
          or silent,
            touched by time).

But the winds
    for this tree
        in its moment of need
can lift a kite
    onto the branches,
        tenderly
(a tree, like a poem, must not think,
                but be).

And while I am shoved
    by lines of force,
the tree conveys to me
    its rooted continuity.

15

All (His Fools)

The bowswain's pipe
wakes the waters,
beckons the unseen sun.
The captain rises
from out the ship,
the ship
from out the sea.

Under orders
for future seas
seamen arc
over helm and scopes
in dark radar rooms
delivering data
for his indelible mind
behind twin-shuttered lamps
flashing at each wave breasted
crested.
And from out these eyes
shoot laser-looks

that capture us
in net-like efficiency.
His lips,
finding each word
preshaped, purposeful,
compel us to fight
or flight
at this demi-god's discretion.
But,
must we sail
on the pool
of his schemes
toward certain catastrophe
till we are all
(his fools)
sinking,
drowning?

16

Forever Emptiness

Once, there were real things:
    nocturnal sounds,
    a lover's soothing lips,
    memories.

Tonight,
    nothing to embrace,
    I stretch my arms full length
    to embrace emptiness
        (my curtain of comfort
        one breath beyond
        infinity's face).

To the music of my instinct,
    I sway,
    the movement
    cause to curve elusive's curtain;
    I speak:
    the words feel that curtain's curves

with shifting forms
    (far beyond
    all purposeful
    syllabic norms).

Forever emptiness
    always near
    forever near,
    and ringing hollow
    at my ear,
    the last sound
    the last sound
        I care to hear.

17

My Father Died on Wednesday

It was, they say,
the doctors' day
off.

I ran
the white span
of the hall;
a hand met
and led me
to his bed.

I could not move
in father's eyes
that tried to soothe
but only
proved me
the colored spot
on all-white-everywhere.

The silence after
was a better thing
than when the sounds came:
gurgles–
    like a faucet
    shut all day
    but now
    would have its say
    before a final emptiness.

18

Gift

Last fall
   I saw a cat
   (so black
      it blazed)
  chimney-sitting
   against
    the buzz-saw sun
     spinning its way
      into the horizon.

But smoke
  and snow
   soon stole
    its vantage point.

Christmas Day
  I found him
   cold
    wrapped in snow

much like a gift
        received.

19

Questions for an Avid Motorcyclist

In the momentary stillness
of the gold blister sun
I stand and watch
the chopper glisten
listen for its piston pulse
as primal as the breast-beat.

I mount the heat
because there is
nothing else.
The tires jerk the distant road
from there to here, then back,
as the sun spins off plexiglass
in a star
while the lance-wind
seeks out every pore
and enters.

My eyelids soon
are sealed by sighs
as if there is
no more to see,

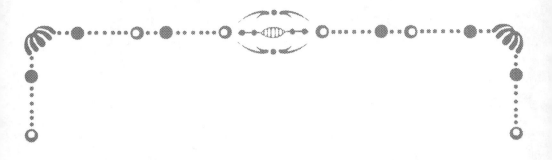

and the way becomes pre-set,
mechanized,
so that
I do not see the explosion
(when it comes),
do not see the pavement
happening in my face,
but intimately know
the shape of pain
as it closes over shattered legs
and moves up.

And then,
there are only questions
in voids of voices;
and I almost see the blood
they, in whispered wonder, awe,
almost feel the broken body
pieced together by interested eyes,
almost begin to question
                    their questions
as sirens come
to sing me sleep.

20

Prometheus – Second Burial

Again,
   always from the southwest
     they come: cyclones, gorged with death
         yet hungry for destruction.

He counts these curls
       (swerving, swirling in ever turning)
    with precision eyes
        set into bronze (eyes
      new-loaned to those alone
         about to die).

Dazed,
  he stays;
     and snatched
      is spun and blown
        flat
       onto the sun to be outlined
     yoked
      suspended in golden
        woven ions.

Predators gather on a cloud-
                branch and grin
      in mirrored sadness
        through spin
          and dancing
            kaleidoscope eyes before
   all wings start
         and circle
    each an eclipse,
    each an answer
     to the prayer of him
      helpless
      held by bonds.

Two vultures plan
   to pierce (without
         a precedent)
    his liver;
their prism beaks collect
         reflect a rainbow sun
   to light his way to darkness.

Stripped bleached unleashed
   his bones tumble free-
           fall

                    into dust
                which rises,
                        swirls,
            then settles like a blanket
            for this unmarked second burial.

21

The Body, Alone

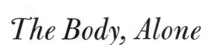

Eleven thirty-three
    under the doorknob, the hole receives the key–
        turned,
            reveals room with sixty-watt bulb
                eleven levels
                    up in a New York City Y.

Desk
    with unused chair, browned and cheap:
        enough!
            A body needs sleep, a chance to forget.
                Phone,
                    black and dumb;

Bible
    and directory, shelved, new from disuse;
        time,
            temperature flashed on window-favored wall;
                winds
                    shake the room, the night.

Sleep
    seizes the surrendering mind;
       night
           finds the room in stone sheathed slumber;
              perfection
                  frowns.

Flames
    infuriated climb eleven stories with the night on fire;
       heat
           melts the man between snow sheets;
              charred,
                  the body, alone...

22

A Child's Eye Rolls Old

In a child's eye
that rolls old,
the pages
of a book
turn round,
and with
a heat
intense
turn crisp
and brown;
and the world
turns too–
makes revolutions
as shifty
as smoke,
as natural
as guns,
as proud
as truth.

The words
blur in heat,
blur
and burn
and turn
in heat;
tears start,
then stop
upon the page
(printed wetness)
curling round
a dying nerve
twitching
quietly, at first,
and then,
no sound.

23

Need Help – Cold

Cloud-clean sky,
desert-sun dry,
blacktop
rides the sand,
and desert cold
flows slow and low
like Passover Plague over
the man stranded
near his car.

Heaters heat,
radios bleat,
and faceless faces glare
through safety glass
in passing cars.
Their slipstreams
beat his face
like insults.
He flaps his arms
to kill the chill
of immobility.

When morning comes
a car hums to a stop
beside the man
sitting stiff
inside his car.
A note in shivered letters
reads

need help
cold
no one cares

24

Wings   *Wings*
Wings

A burst of flapping, rapid
  Above the waters, slightly
    Across the sun, darkened
      by the mighty burst of wings.

For those who never flew   I
  describe the scene;
    For those who had the wings,
      but would not,
        could not try
          to fly,   I
 describe the sound:
      the thunder
        the brilliance
          of the flight.

For those who did not try,   I
  will fly

beyond the reach of doubt,
beyond the touch of pain,
beyond the feel of fear,
until I'm home again.

Once again I'll tell the story
that I flew
to those who

chose to forget,

but always knew...

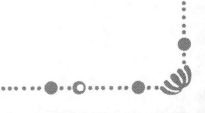

25

Harmonic Convergence:
A New Beginning

It started with the light:

Force without form,
like breath repressed:

contractions
expanding,
dispersing;

a nova
soon saddened
by space
and time

until,

too far
from the Source

all this
we call
life

stops.

26

Touched, Turned on till Worn out

The last poem *Touch, Turned on Till Worn out* is the last poem submitted by the author as it is; damaged and hard to read. It tells the finale of the author's experience. Margaret Howell, the writer of the Foreword and Iqbal Coddington, the point of contact decided it is symbolic to include this poem in the book for interested readers who might be able to decipher it. If so, it will be greatly appreciated to send a copy of it to the publisher and added to the future collection of the author's poems.

Printed in the United States
By Bookmasters